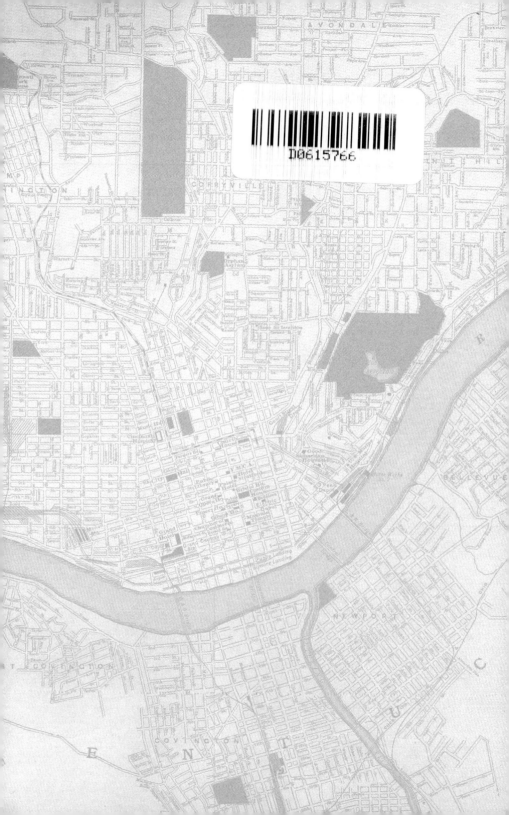

IMMEDIATE SONG

IMMEDIATE SONG

Poems

DON BOGEN

MILKWEED EDITIONS

Published 2019 by Milkweed Editions
Printed in the United States of America
Cover design by Mary Austin Speaker
Cover illustration: *The Rand-McNally New Commercial Atlas Map of Cincinnati and Environs, Cincinnati,* 1912
Author photo by Claudia Monpere
19 20 21 22 23   5 4 3 2 1
First Edition

Milkweed Editions, an independent nonprofit publisher, gratefully acknowledges sustaining support from the Ballard Spahr Foundation; the Jerome Foundation; the McKnight Foundation; the National Endowment for the Arts; the Target Foundation; and other generous contributions from foundations, corporations, and individuals. Also, this activity is made possible by the voters of Minnesota through a Minnesota State Arts Board Operating Support grant, thanks to a legislative appropriation from the arts and cultural heritage fund, and a grant from Wells Fargo. For a full listing of Milkweed Editions supporters, please visit milkweed.org.

Library of Congress Cataloging-in-Publication Data

Names: Bogen, Don, author.
Title: Immediate song : poems / Don Bogen.
Description: First edition. | Minneapolis, Minnesota : Milkweed Editions,
   2019.
Identifiers: LCCN 2018032685 (print) | LCCN 2018035247 (ebook) | ISBN
   9781571319449 (ebook) | ISBN 9781571314819 (pbk. : alk. paper)
Classification: LCC PS3552.O4337 (ebook) | LCC PS3552.O4337 A6 2019 (print) |
   DDC 811/.54--dc23
LC record available at https://lccn.loc.gov/2018032685

Milkweed Editions is committed to ecological stewardship. We strive to align our book production practices with this principle, and to reduce the impact of our operations in the environment. We are a member of the Green Press Initiative, a nonprofit coalition of publishers, manufacturers, and authors working to protect the world's endangered forests and conserve natural resources. *Immediate Song* was printed on acid-free 30% postconsumer-waste paper by Versa Press.

For Ted, Anna, Garrett, and Sam

In memory of Cathryn

CONTENTS

I

ON HOSPITALS

i. Grounds

The old ones held a varnished elegance
like mansions, cruise ships, or resort hotels—
quiet places, formal, set apart.

You dressed up when you visited. The ease
of a leisured past gleamed in their rooms:
the vaulted lobby with mahogany desk,

mail slots, and leather chairs where I waited
with my father for my sisters to be born;
the long, open TB porch in the Harz;

or the solarium at Cowell where my wife
had mono as a student. Each morning
she'd wake to cortisone and fresh orange juice,

a view of campus in the lifting haze:
damp redwoods, eucalyptus, and the steam
of coffee rising from a china cup.

ii. A Run

Taxpayer opulence, generous care—
a quaint nostalgia, I know, no room for it
now everything is sleeked-down, corporate,

high-tech: medical centers with landscaping,
tasteful signage listing doctors as groups
and associates, intricate as law firms.

The buildings themselves have shrunk, reproduced,
and spread out into complexes, like the one
I run through sometimes: a hospital village

suffused on Sunday mornings with village quiet.
I pass the closed clinics and rehab centers,
construction sites abandoned for the day,

garages almost empty, night nurses
slumping at the bus shelter in scrubs
like washed-out pajamas. Few visitors

at this hour—but once I saw a boy
walking behind his mother, in new shoes,
bow tie, and stiff blue suit, carrying a rose.

It snags the heart, that helpless love of the child
who fears the parent may leave too soon, helpless
parent afraid to leave the child too soon

(it is always too soon). The hospital
holds these feelings like a theater,
an album flush with memories, a brain.

iii. Rooms

There are rooms for arrival—the green-tiled vault
where our daughter met the world, the lustrous hall
buzzing with student doctors for our son—

and rooms for departure, with their tanks and screens,
tangled nests of tubes, and endless humming
as if you were inside a clock. When age

thumps on your heart, thickens your blood, they need
for you to drink this grayish milkshake now.
Here is a cap for your newly bald head,

a gown that ties in the back where you can't reach.
Your IV stand, a frail hat rack on wheels,
will accompany you—slowly, slowly—

to the awkward bathroom. Everyone here
is nice but distant, everyone in these rooms
is tired but cannot sleep. Because you're old

you are a child again, like everyone here,
taking your medicine from a little cup,
trying hard to figure out how to please.

iv. Promise

This is for your own good—no way to say that,
carrying our son back to the hospital
each morning for a week after his birth:

from the freezing car through tunnels (warmer now,
his eyelids starting to flutter, lips to suck)
to a waiting room, an office with a nurse

who jabbed his heel—and you cried, you cried,
my sallow one. No way to tell our daughter
the X-ray machine adjusting its black beak

above her skull wouldn't hurt. Or that hurt might help,
as in my childhood, when curtains in the gym
were placed so that we couldn't see the nurse

with alcohol, cotton balls, and fresh vaccine,
the needles in wooden trays like silverware.
We knew one of the boys would pass out,

some girls would cry, in this ritual we performed
one day in fall and again the following year
so we might all escape the iron lung.

Public health. The clinic had marble stairs
and cheerful wood blocks in the waiting room,
a brisk lady doctor, good with children

(dedicated, I'd like to think, not just
shunted off here), whom my mother chose
to give me the earliest vaccinations,

who looked in my ears with a tiny light,
listened to my breathing, tapped my knee,
asked questions, answered those my mother had,

and wrote out the prescription, showing by this
how all of us could meet our needs: the lost
gleaming promise of the welfare state.

v. Media Studies

Hospitals look better on TV,
with hunky interns, music, and tight plots:
the drug-addicted nurse, bubonic plague

a greasy terrorist keeps brandishing
in a vial. Threats, then safety, and the news
at eleven. Now the hospital moves

offscreen a while, a last phase after the shootout
or freeway chase. Heroic-medic scenes
with hospitals in jungles, mountain huts,

bombed-out cities, or field camps on the edge
of the latest rubble-strewn battlefield
add glamour to the show. But who would go

to the hospital in real life, given a choice?
We're scared of the procedures and costs,
the bad news they may carry—a load of pain

that grows, a narrowed future—so we hide
until the ambulance comes to scoop us up.
A run of tests, intensive care, and then

the quick skid to the slab. Hospitals
keep a special place for this downstairs,
cold storage in the basement, the whole building

a funnel to the morgue. Vertical coffins,
corpse silos, boxes of the grimmest facts,
their towers suggest the long odds stacked against us.

vi. Flags

In the first years after college, friends found work
in towers linked to these: the labyrinths
of medical insurance. Hall on hall

of monitors and keyboards, padded headsets,
and hidden clocks for time-motion studies.
Data on them was being entered as

they entered data. Layers of observation
stacked up like the cases on their screens.
Trying to flag each doubtful claim, as they'd

been trained, they were flags themselves, placed in
between things: a warning left inside
the doctor's file, extra lid on the pill jar,

bar on the hospital door—part of a dam
diverting the stream of illness and its care
to drive the whirling turbines of commerce.

vii. Compañero

English majors (Systems Managers there),
they never lasted very long. Who would
enjoy having to function as a block

day after frustrating day? I suspect
even the soldiers delaying the ambulance
that carried Neruda to the hospital

in the first days of the coup didn't want
to tilt up the bed, search it for weapons,
and check the passengers' papers. The man

was dying, they could see that, and no threat.
Because they followed orders he suffered more.
He had an everyday incurable cancer

and kept on fighting against the blocked-up world
with rage and humor, calling himself the Great
Urinator, inviting Nixonicide.

Pharmacy, church of the desperate,
with a little god in every pill,
often you are too expensive, the price

of the medicine closes your clear doors,
and the poor go back, jaws clenched, to the dark room
of staying sick. May the day arrive

when you'll be free, no longer peddling hope,
and the victories of life, all human life,
over great death will be your victories.

viii. A Joke

A guy goes into a hospital with stage-one
melanoma on his arm, has it removed,
and asks the doctor—Lebanese, from Beirut,

with olive skin, black hair, and wet brown eyes
wild as Ernie Kovacs's—how to prevent
another cancerous mole. A one-beat pause,

then: *Have genes like mine?* A break for laughs,
a handshake, and the doctor leaves the room,
the braces on his shoes thumping the floor.

The body is a weight the hospital
can help us lift. And it's a kind of clock
the hospital tries to read. There are times

preset in your cells, when things will get
interesting: tests in special rooms,
cameras snaked inside you, you inside

a beige machine that magnetizes you
and clanks. How late is it? My turn now?
Even the gorgeous rich who can afford

trainers to help polish their good fortune
have a particular spot in that waiting line
and never can be certain where it is.

ix. Dictionary

Hospital, from *hospes*, a guest or host.
Neither stays very long at the *hospitale*,
or inn. Administrators leave at five,

patients are discharged, and doctors zip
between wards and their offices in the world
like scouting bees. The buildings themselves imply

the temporary, with curtains, partitions
instead of walls, and multipurpose rooms.
Wings open up and shut down, entrances

are swallowed as exteriors become
interiors that don't quite fit, and age
cracks out through paint and plaster till at last

the whole structure is smashed by wrecking balls,
or picked apart, or imploded as we watch
on TVs that might as well be screens

charting our own collapse. The hospital,
then, as heap of rubble, *memento mori*,
a transient guesthouse housing transients.

x. Sealed Rooms

Sometimes there are unexpected stays—
in Toronto, in Guangzhou. Hospital
as prison suddenly, the inn locked down,

and liberation comes at calendar pace.
To question every breath, each fluctuation
of body heat, and wait. And waiting, think

how time opens some wards and seals off others,
cuts to the chase or seeps into your bones—
relentless, uncomfortable meditation

the hospital and your fears have boxed you in.
What virus will hop next from the stacked cages
to the kitchen, that plane you took, your bed?

When it catches up with you, will you be caught
on a locked floor? Or wandering alone
in the dead-end maze of managed care?

xi. Wheels

Nightmares, real and imagined—just telling them
consoles and half-prepares me for bad news.
But it's indulgent too, as when I see

the warning signs with their black steer-horn points
on latched cases in the examining room
and wonder: If I put my hand inside,

what would I pick up? Curiosity
starts spinning its little wheel that makes the big
wheel turn. Grim causes leading to their grim

effects—but also plans and hopes, new ways
to meet our needs, some victory perhaps
over great death. The old funicular

lurches. We rise through fog and thinning pines.
Odd dreams peek out, regrets, scenes from the past,
disconnected facts glaring, then lost

in clouds that fade as everything at last
comes clear: It's true Herr Castorp is ill—
why would he spend time up here otherwise?

xii. Windows

When I stop again and look up from the page,
staring out across the bare tree limbs
above the neighbors' roofs, I see the tower

of Good Samaritan Hospital. Today
someone in the children's ward has taped
folded-paper snowflakes, big as hands,

across a strip of windows. Scissor-cut,
symmetrical, they magnify a dream
of winter joy outdoors for those who have

to stay inside. From this distance they seem
like real snowflakes, just a gauzy blur.
But up close on my window I see ice-dots

and small white leaves that melt against the pane,
spreading a screen of drizzle between me
and the cheerful nurses there. Cheerful?

I can't know that, but why not imagine
children's needs—or anyone's—at the inn
where most of us will stop one day? I'd like

the nurses cheerful as they move through halls
where someone took the time to think about
the color of the paint. I want the hours

unrushed, the doctors calm, the children
warm, well cared for, ready to come home
in just a day or two.

II

RETURN SONG

How could I mourn?
Time cleansed the town,
scouring to brightness
what had looked gray.

High city hall
at the head of its plaza,
church like a mission
with courts and arcades.

Where did I walk?
Through a rinsed past:
bungalows, old parks,
old Spanish names.

Street of the Oaks,
Street of the Mill,
Street of the Big House,
our small house there.

What did I find?
The porch with an arbor,
the chipped stucco wall
renewed in white paint.

The view of the mountains
more clear, more distant,
my parents suspended
inside memory.

Whom did I seek then?
Ash in the sea,
drifting in thin silt
some miles away.

CARE SONG

Who will take care of the boy
who has no need of care?
The parents' caring now
useless as the shroud
and roses in the dirt.

Who will console the child
who cannot hear a word?
The family's wounded calls
faltering in air—
who will answer now?

How will the brother find
his way in empty dawns,
the lengthening chain of days
entwining him, the dark
that will not set him free?

When the father sobs,
caught by a bedroom door,
and the mother bears
a migraine in her eyes,
how will the boy comfort them?

How will he speak to us
in dreams fading with light,
in memories that dim
and deepen in our care,
now he must live there?

HOUSE

A high level of housing construction and vigorous community development
are essential to the economic and social well being of our country.
—DWIGHT D. EISENHOWER, 1954

Schmidt made me
Like others each in turn as the street grew south
I was a pit in clay
A wall of cinder block holding out the damp
My parts began diverging, my purposes cleared
I was tar and poured cement
I was a skeleton of two-by-fours, the wind between my ribs

Floorboards gave me layers
Men stood on them, smoking cigarettes
Boys climbed down ladders to explore my partitions
I was a concert of hammering, band saws whined at my perimeters
My horizon was a battlefield of trenches and stakes
Schmidt's truck kept bringing my devices
Pipes for fluids, wires to connect me with the world

I was plaster, I was rubber and glass
My joists, my iron ligaments grew invisible
I took on angles, gable and dormer and plumb back door
I blocked the wind, I was rooms each linked to another
Ducts and vents gave me unity
Women came, their hands on my walls
I was whitewash and would be paint and would wear cloth

Around me my brothers stood up in the field
Only the oldest trees were taller
Fresh asphalt welcomed Schmidt's truck, marked my border

Sidewalk traveled beside it
I support habitation, my green robe is growing
My arms extend to every corner
At my heart new sheet metal sings in the heat

MAILBOX

White, aluminum, shaped like a loaf of bread
It rises on a two-by-four
In front of the weeds and plank fence across the street
Standing in isolation and near obsolescence
Against the green below and weathered brown-gray behind

Its flag, stiff as the one on the moon, is unlifted
Its door, when you open it
Becomes a slide, a shelf, an extension of the cool ridged floor
A slick-covered magazine is sleeping facedown
With a local flyer rolled tight by a rubber band

On top of them, letters, in a stack still neat
From when the carrier squared them against her palm
Bills with their transparent address windows and metered tops
Fat packets of bulk-rate solicitation full of coupons and offers
Prepaid envelopes for your immediate reply

Never to be given, never to be considered even
The whole stack dropped easily in the recycling bin
One last stage in the web of hoped-for interaction
From your hand back to the carrier's, to truck driver and deft sorting clerk
Designer and copywriter at their bright screens dreaming up campaigns

The metal house is empty again, its door shut, privacy restored
Even its absurdity and cheapness hold a tinge of sorrow still
Receptacle of loneliness, of lost dreams, connections rejected
Its post the same shade as the fence behind it
It seems to float in air

SMART SONG

He tops the pine,
        swaying the last branch,
and stares me down
        from that perch.

As if he sensed
        my jagged unease,
he wants me out
        of this new place

in the sea wind
        and clarifying light—
I'm stopped cold
        by his taunt.

How can one crow
        raise these old fears?
Beauty and calm
        seem part of the air.

You're nowhere now,
        his call cuts my heart.
So smart, so smart,
        you think you're so smart.

LAKE SONG

Drove to the lake and the lake was cold
The whole town grim in gray morning light
Harbor abandoned, coal boats gone
Walked on the gritty beach, shuffled among
Mussel shells, driftwood, algae, feathers
Jumped over creeks spilling from drainpipes
Found clay beach stones that broke at a touch

Walked on the pier and the pier was long
Under the cloud cap, swirling and blank
No gulls swooping, no shrieks in the gusts
Gray water darkened as the pier stretched on
Whitecaps rising, wind in my eyes
The pocked concrete wet, sides piled with big rocks
Fish bones in crevices, old hooks, snagged line

Came to the lighthouse and the house was sealed
Stood on the walkway two feet from the waves
Looked to the south where the power plant loomed
North to the point and west to the town
Looked east to the layers, fog-gray, mist-white
Blankets diffusing the cold sun's sheen
Saw what I could and could not see

DESKS

Old papers, old stationery, I know, in the heavy drawers
With filigreed brass pulls that dropped and clanged when you opened them
Everything stuffed in there: letters, bills, odd wallet-sized photos
Dried-out pens nestled along the edges of the ruffled piles
Shifting textures of paper, stiff plastic, and cardboard in different weights
Address books, old calendars, an envelope full of checks,
      announcements from businesses

All of these clamoring in their mute voices
Print under logos, typing that showed where a finger slipped or a key caught
The loopy handwriting of my mother before she got sick
Filling the space between the light-blue lines on the folded pages
My mother, or my grandmother—which paper, which desk, where
The bright dining room or the dim one, neither much used

I can choose at will, I can pull at the tight drawers and work them open
The handles clattering, the crammed-in papers expanding a bit, as if able
      to breathe
I am comfortable now, my ballpoint fluent, I am reading what I see
I look up from each desk and find either small, gold-framed pictures, a
      ballerina under glass
And a stack of paid bills wrapped with a rubber band
Or a light brown wall where memory has neglected to set anything

Through four generations it has gone on fading, it has never been repainted
Because it's near the archway to the living room, light barely reaches it
The other desk splits light, dispensing it among the photos and geegaws
The mountains are nearby, they loom over the shoulder of someone
      writing there
Who is a ghost, lost, absorbed in a task and thus fully alive
Paying no attention to her desk or the others

FLOWERS IN A VASE

The dahlias' unopened buds poke like periscopes above their clownish mass
Green-yellow-red ranks of petals peel back around the hungry centers
Their bent-open invitations frame a pillow of seed
The long stems are drinking straws, the leaves a simple engine of sunlight
I understand their mechanics which will end soon

They droop in the vase now: cut, sterile, a blazon
That slashes the white apartment walls, the leather couch, all the tastefulness
My gaze moves like an art student's between them and a pad of paper
Their repeated gestures look intricate and foreign
Blatant life, oblivious to its strategies, assaults the eye

After a day their water grows murky as turtles'
Blowsy, blown, they will keep on fading whether I change it or not
A waxy perfume exudes from them
Nothing will complete their purposes here
They have no point to make but they shout

III

A CITIZEN

It's true I lived in the twilight of empire,
the glow at the center already muffled in rumor,
the provinces indistinct, conspiratorial,
alliances like sand falling through the tired fingers of diplomats
while the orators held forth endlessly in the splendor of their halls.
Yet many believed grand days were still ahead of us—
and how, in this, were we different from any age?

There were the usual cabals,
careers to be made among court intrigues
as the wheels of dynasty ground slowly through a calendar of ceremonies.
Slaves peeked out from invisibility from time to time—
an eye, an open mouth, an arm raised then subdued—
and we knew of warrens near the public temples
where plague ruled and flesh was coinage.
But laws and executions gave us a sense of protection,
and there were holidays and amusements,
abundance in the markets for those who had means of exchange,
and tribute still coming in along our fabled roads.

At the outposts, war on small war—
so many, when I think back I lose track of them all:
incursions in the forests, seizures of islands,
fiefdoms defended or toppled among odd sects in the desert.
We took our reports from the centurions
and, when we weren't too busy or tired of it all,
discussed the day-to-day triumphs of the legions abroad.

We knew the most important concerns are close to home.
Our vineyards were narrow but well cultivated,
our marriages reasonable.

Faced with confusion, we were content to wait through it.
We placed our trust in character and good management.
Like others, we had our gods and offerings,
our games of chance, the oracles with their mysteries.
When we thought about the future, we saw our goals
as shimmering ideals, simple and universally shared
except by those who wished to do us harm.
We were a generous people and kept our hearts open.

A NOTEBOOK

In these foreign lands   they will see how we build our houses,
they will see with their own eyes   how we earn our bread.
—EL CANTAR DE MIO CID

I wanted to write something about the flags there.
Pennants in a clanking harbor, their clean colors brightening the sky,
wind ornaments, calls over distances, beacons, prayers
for fishermen just coming in with the dawn's catch, for sailboats, yachts,
and the fireboats and rescue ships looking out for them all—
each morning in that small port on the Mediterranean
these banners lifted my heart.
I wanted to sketch their billowing changes
and my own good fortune in being there to see them.
Yet all around me, though I hardly noticed them
in the strict light of that exotic place,
were the flags of nations, with their imperial symbology:
a cross, keys, tower, stars, a slit moon, bundle of sticks tied with a cord.
They floated there in abstraction—assertion, dream, rule, threat—
driving toward perpetuity in everything they claimed.

———

I remember the flag in that church painting.
Because the map was changing and the country needed a myth,
the saint took on a special banner and a new name:
on horseback, James, now Santiago Matamoros,
displays a small battle pennant decorated with scallop shells.
His face is blank and slightly girlish,
his body enclosed in a carapace of armor
like a shiny beetle propped upright on a stallion.

From his free hand, a blade dangles,
beneath it the lopped heads of his enemies, bug-eyed, stunned,
round as bowling balls festooned with Turkish mustachios
(a Gothic version, the painter having never seen a Moor).
The saint looks bored—he is clearly beyond this—
preacher, faith healer, martyred apostle
dragged back to earth to crank up the Reconquest.

———

What is the comparison between these two photographs:
the marine hunched and weeping after saying good-bye to his daughter,
the Iraqi boy wounded, gauze wrapped loosely around his neck?
Reduced to raw feeling, both pictures draw us to the eyes:
the marine's stunned, on the edge of despair, the Iraqi boy's dark slits.
Delicacy of eyelashes, beating, almost imperceptibly,
and the shallow cups of bone protecting the places where the brain
        gathers light,
the fragile globes of fluids and nerves,
their lenses tuned to all around them so miraculously.
The camera pulls us to these wet surfaces of the face
we would question, we would console,
reflections of our own eyes imagined inside them—
O human forms divine.

———

Blake chatting naked in his garden with Mrs. Blake,
autodidact, draughtsman, seer of visions, certifiably mad,
in the tame south London summer, streaks of cloud and changing shadows,
narrating heavenly wars, illuminating the villains,

their stiff white beards and cracked eyes, lined muscles, merciless limbs,
who haunt—he saw in his madness—the world in which we live,
world of empires advancing, of famine, plague, the hapless soldier's sigh
splattered across the walls of ancient cities.

———

The Library is in their path
Beautiful thing! aflame.

Parchment, papyrus, rag paper—all the ingenious surfaces
that keep words light and lasting:
black ash caught in the updrafts.

Beautiful thing! aflame.

And the outsides transforming more slowly,
blisters on calfskin, holes in smoldering cloth
expanding till the bright tongues leap from their hearts.

Beautiful thing! aflame.

Law codes, old Torahs, a much-copied doctor's manual
from the capital of Western learning at Córdoba—
soldier, looter, arsonist, commander,

The Library is in their path
Beautiful thing! aflame.

———

The boxes are rough because there are so many, and because of the hurry.
The pit is open and beginning to fill.
The boxes are narrow,
each laid out in front of a number on a sheet.
Workers are scurrying—the photo can't show weeping in another room.
Because the image of God is forbidden, writing itself becomes illumination:
on each plywood lid a name swooping in black paint,
simple identification as prayer.
The boxes will be moved from the pit when the shelling is over,
but now they have their place in the history of collective retribution,
one family caught driving away from their house in Tyre.

———

In the country of water, between two rivers,
valley of green crops staving off the sand,
country of cities ancient as trade
and the first words cut into stone to record it,
birthplace of the patriarch, of tribal dreams,
a garden called paradise where four rivers flowed,
a garden hanging from palace walls,
country of empire, of exile and slavery,
of towers like all towers marking power, achievement, pride,
under stars recorded and studied for five thousand years,
on earth worked into fertility even longer,
by these waters I sat down and wept.

———

I remember taking the flag down and carrying it in when I worked at the
    post office
in the dry heat of summer, the jungle war overrunning our TVs,
how it had to be folded a certain way, with triangular flips and neat
    undertucks,
as it would be outside the Capitol, or at a Scout meeting,
or at an airstrip over coffins about to be shipped home.
Rattle of that flagpole where the town met the parched arroyos
as the Santa Ana began to pick up near the end of August, threatening fire,
rattle of that blank mast, rope, and pulley, like a snake met alone on a
    canyon path,
like knucklebones kept as souvenirs in a hollowed-out skull.

————

War as the blind pig rooting, rooting,
wet snout pushing up craters, foxholes, berms,
snuffling, dismembering, scattering wreckage and blood,
its forefeet stiff hoofed balances, neck a shaft,
digging for what is buried—what, anything, it doesn't know—
not hunting, not scavenging, just thrusting and ingesting,
all touch and instinct, everything turned over, pushed apart,
pressing on, pressing, innocent and relentless.
Who set the studded collar on that stub of neck?
Who, standing back a bit, holds the leash?

————

Another emblem there! The man on the box,
wires dangling from the fingertips of his half-drooping extended arms,
the hood giving his head a strained, searching pose.
Two triangles, then, a small one capping a large,
on a little stalk set awkwardly on a pedestal.
Dark Christmas tree, scarecrow, crucifix, sheeted ghost—
terrible this rush to metaphor, escape into simplification and irony.
Terrible the minds dreaming up the scene in all its intricacy,
from the blinding to the phony wires and sad exposed feet,
advised by doctors, free to act as the quick will decides
in the service of an assertion, service of building up fear
that makes the muscles tighten, the sphincter release—
I am trying to draw a line across this icon,
I am trying to take my hands off the wires.

IN THE RAIN

A man who lives in his car
bathes in rainwater.
The wrinkles on his face
are streaking black, a loose
T-shirt slaps his skin.
Dripping, near the storm drain,
he sheds one coat of grime
among many anointing him.

His home is a Plymouth coupe
broad as a boat. He keeps
one of everything there:
one narrow bicycle tire,
sunglasses with one lens
missing, a bent umbrella,
a caulking gun, one stuffed
blue rhinoceros.

Looking around the street,
he scratches, soaks, and waits.
At night he'll go to work
as always, stopping to check
the dumpsters in back lots
of closed supermarkets,
sorting street trash. Now, though,
there's nothing for him to do

but bathe. A driver's stare
slides off him like the fears
he first saw long ago:
no people but walking ghosts,

no dogs but grubs with teeth,
the park a dark arena
for the trial of his soul—
all sinking into swirls

that vanish down the drain.
They will be back again
like hunger and dirt,
but the rain lets him forget.
He wants it to come down
in flooding curtains now,
he wants it to keep on
a good long time.

STREET, WINDOW

Car life: net of plans, chores, news on the radio
Bubbles of glare streak the vista
Walkers take longer, eyes leading the pace

Ahead for the café, down for dogshit, left for speeding taxis
That brain rocking slightly in its bath of senses, this one still
What he wrote in a glass case

They rode the bus, a box of windows
On her way somewhere—the café, the bookstore, anywhere I want
Air, glass, air, wool, cotton, rayon, skin

That time you spent with me cut off from life
City ant-like, swarming, like an anthill, swarming with ants
When I leaf through the dictionary I am hiding

He always had to wear sunglasses, even when the sky was gray
Garage doors lifting and closing slow eyelids
The brick part is mute, the corrugated metal tagged and boasting

In the windows lace or gauze, a scrim
She would enact anything but resisted contact with her mouth
A sound like surf, waves passing as the lights change

Horns of different pitch and duration: car sighs, car shouts
What the eye takes in I narrow
One who strolls or ambles purposelessly

Stick, cane, crutches, walker, wheelchair
In the map book a fat yellow line, divided
Sign with a signpost, door with a doorguard

After a while there was more to see with the shutters closed
Depends which room has a light on

OUR MUTUAL FRIEND

That he could see the great wheel in its turning
as it drew out the eccentrics he had found
along his winding night walks; that its whirling,
rough as it was then, hurling to the ground
an entrepreneurial god or jolting up
a trash collector, pulsed inside his bones
and drove the engine of his mind to keep
gathering, dreaming, arranging, bringing home
the thief, the saint, the earnest awkward youth,
witch, fool, and miser quickened into lines
of script, then type, a passion sweeping through
the vast rhetorical windstorms of his scenes
that sing now like a train well underway,
defining the landscape with its energy.

DANCE

Three on three below street level, partners changing
Dance of hip pocket, breast pocket, hand in the pocket
Hand slipped through the unzipped slit on the backpack
Dance of touch, subtle clutch, pressed contact almost erotic
Of a day's work, of fending off an attack of bees

In the low tunnels full of echoes and cries
On platforms by brief open doors, furtive in plain sight
Dance of quick slippage, silk, leather, fingertips
Three on three like a shell game and where is the wallet
Afloat on a dance of hands, pocket to pocket to sack

Dance of skilled distraction, of improv
Steps, glances, gestures threaded in the surge
A tango, a slow grope, impudent flamenco
Time its fluid master, survival its reward
Dance cut short by the closing doors, by a shout

DIAMOND SONG

The band is loud, its firm bass thumps
    the heart and will not stop.
Off to the side, we nod and mime
    as she comes bounding up.

What dance is this that cuts her knees
    and makes her elbows point,
riffling her, as if she were
    a marionette?

The body slips to let joy loose
    when it moves to the beat.
But her joy is taut and pure,
    beyond the bass line's reach.

Her torso sleek with energy,
    jittery yet sure,
is following the sharpened pulse
    from another room.

I catch it in her glossy eyes
    that can't stay long with mine
but dart their cold sparks all around
    as if somewhere inside

her bobbing skull a diamond sliced
    across a whirling disk.
Why don't I feel the music now?
    What dance is this?

PROMISE SONG

When the taps ran blood
     she set her books on fire—
then she was in a white place
     where everyone lied.

Words, words, words:
     smoke puffed out from mouths,
stick figures of her name
     in riot on the forms.

The fat door hides the rules
     under its mattress pad.
A conference room is calm.
     If you promise, they said,

and told me in the silence
     after they put her back,
Don't listen—everything
     she tells you is a lie.

IV

AFTER SOME YEARS

The mind
is an impermanent place, isn't it,
but it looks to permanence.
—THOM GUNN

I like to remember him
among a city crowd,
that jagged, dazzling flow
outside of offices
and sealed, oblivious cars.
He'd plunge into the stream,
a part of it, his eye
alive to each detail,
the body trim and quick,
good boots to hit the street—
then home, where he would read
like a grad student.

He kept a certain edge
of tension when we met:
a touch of the young man,
his mind on other things,
ready to take off fast
if conversation dulled.
I miss that sense of risk.
Its spikiness stood out
against the normal blur
of comfortable, safe talk.

Nothing safe appealed
to him—he'd slip away.
But once his will had seized
on something worth his full
attention, he could be
relentless in pursuit.
A line just slightly off,
an argument unresolved,
a capsule that might hone
the eyes all night or drop
the mind into a dank
oubliette—he'd keep
up with it, keep on
holding what held him,
wrestling with the god
he'd chosen to take on.

I see him walking home,
starting to sort the loot
he's gathered from the night,
working it, looking right
into it, as fog
pearls with morning sun.
It's not hard to imagine
a version of that same
tenacity in bars:
within the jostling flux,
the heart set to the beat,
the body testing itself
over and over in time,
all its fine bold moves
accustomed to surprise,
reliable and firm.

How long could it have held?
I can't picture the months
he stared into the dark,
watching each man's slow fall:
loss of strength, weight, sight—
then beds and breathing tubes.
In sheeted rooms he felt
the aching hook of hope
and bleak routine of care.
A letter arrived:
My time of grief is done,
all my friends are dead.

How to reply to that?
I couldn't then, and still
find myself shifting
to easier memories.
Like Cole Street, where love
held a whole household:
their kitchen schedule, work
and gifts each gave in turn—
a *boisterous* group, I'd say,
to use a word he liked—
a table up for hours
with laughter and wild talk,
the view out over roofs,
drawings along the hall
that led to separate rooms,
in one of which he died.

It saddens me to think
he shut his door on them.
If his strength of will

betrayed him in the end—
quick promise of the drug
sealed across his face,
the muscles' vibrant jolt,
the heart stuck in its track—
could that be called a choice?

I'll never answer that.
What I want, I know,
is some transcendent note,
one defining scene
rendering him at last
into an ordered past,
which he would hate. His face
stares at me from a sketch,
a map of red-brown lines,
fading, intricate.
Things change, feelings too,
even about the dead.
Nothing will be fixed,
nothing set.

ELEGIES

What comes more easily now
than writing to the dead?

To look back at the body
and tell what it would know

(if it were still someone
who could know) consoles,

the slowly gathered pain
harmonious as snow.

You did, *You were* float down
and melt on the closed lids.

You would—subjunctive, pure—
drifts upward in cold fog.

The list keeps lengthening.
Name after name, each gets

a little heap of songs:
white prayers, white offerings,

a shabby vanity
the dark will wash away.

ARCHAEOLOGY OF 1956

Temple

You must show dignity, you are entering a sacred place
Up four steps past columns, through the heavy gold-bordered doors
Onto echoing marble, but hushed now—dignity, dignity
By the distances, calm men in suits, and dark oak wainscoting
Victorian, clubby, curt, demanding even in memory
Behind the tellers' cages a glimpse of the vault astounds you
The door a round steel wall, its thick bolts gray, pneumatic
Open now—the whole high-ceilinged enterprise open late on Fridays
To accept and protect your paycheck, all of your paychecks then
A teller behind bars takes it along with your little book, sober as a passport
Thumps them with rubber stamps and hands back a few bills
Tokens of your encounter with the powers

Market

Out into the street, alive with crowds of others like you
Young parents with young children, the boom still expanding
Past the city park with its popcorn stand, war memorial, and fountain of
    mineral water staining the concrete brown
The four-story department store offering everything any one of you
    could ever need
Food, shoes, underwear, sewing patterns, bed sets
And the small enticing catalogue outlets for Sears Roebuck and
    Montgomery Ward
Into the dime store where bridge mix and chocolate-covered peanuts
    glimmer dully behind glass
Combs, charm bracelets, and flip-flops jostle in the shallow open bins
The lunch counter is closed, a stand with a poster for hot beef
    sandwiches blocks the entrance
Parakeets whistle and chirp in the back near the radios
Such cheap abundance, so many families weaving around the thin aisles
You are in there and it is all gone and there is nothing I can't remember

Palace

Rex, Majestic—these are the names of theaters
They sing their faded claims now to dim boxes with the seats sold off
Memory prowls a foyer past the velvet rope
Up the broad, thick-carpeted stairs—not dignity but elegant indulgence
To the lounge, the balcony for smokers where it can place you at last
It is paradise up here, the speakers are close
You sit near the big side lamps like torches pointing up
To an ocean of stylized constellations engulfing the ceiling
More names: Academy, Lyric, Alhambra, State
Kingdoms of stucco, domed capitols, resurgence of Athens or
       al-Andalus, places you would never see
Everything in these show halls conspiring to escape the Friday-night
       main street
As ravaged and abandoned now as they are

WINDOW SONG

Leaf green and lichen,
* moss green on bark*

Light rain in the wind
outlines him on the tree:
dark where it's wet now,
a green man on a limb,
his hair as in a carving
made with three blunt strokes,
a prophet's beard in runnels
covering his mouth.
The eyes small, staring
a little to the left,
suggest a world of cares.
I watch him through a screen:
green man on a gray limb
in the dripping air.

Gray man on a green limb
now that the rain has stopped.
In the clearing air,
as the green turns light,
he blurs into the limb,
the man becoming tree,
the tree itself again.
His beard trails to the knot
where a branch fell off.
Birds sing in his face—
his features grow confused.
In the wind that lifts

rain clouds from my sight
the outline fades from view.

Leaf green and lichen,
moss green on bark

MOVING SONG

White sky, dry white air,
      cars in glinting lines.
Near Riverside my breath went tight—
      my father swerved through lanes

into a drugstore parking lot.
      Wheezing in the glare
that sealed my shrinking cage of glass,
      I watched the sliding door

and counted palms along the street.
      I was afraid to move.
Time balked. Our trek across eight states
      began to blur. I knew

I had to wait. If I could wait
      calmly and not lose
control of what I knew—our car,
      my count, my mother's voice—

then I . . . My rigid lungs were sprayed
      with cold mist from a tube,
to open like exotic flowers
      in that blanched afternoon.

SOFT SONG

Look at the soft rain
sifting straight down,
soaking the moss
on the top of the wall.

Look at the stained bricks
taking it in,
the chips, cracks, and flaws
all darkening.

Damp mortar is crumbling
in grains fine as silt
so slowly no one
can follow it.

Above, on new branches
water beads build
to fall like berries
full of wet light.

Such cycles, such gleaming
and gradual loss—
I've studied for hours
behind smudged glass.

The quick whisperings
too faint now to hear—
what did they tell me,
all those years?

THE ICE RINK

They dazzle me still, those teenagers of the fifties slow-skating arm in arm
Under the high lights that made the rest of the park look darker
The speakers on the wired poles sing to them
They are in love with the wordless *ah*s and *ooh*s
The earnest falsetto, the bass man's pledge over the bridge
Their blade strokes slight and silent, their feet barely move
Scarves dangle from their shoulders, there are pom-poms above her ears
Their unimaginable secrets make white puffs near their faces
Brief as the glances when their eyes meet
They circle the rink slowly as the record circles its spindle
And glide for a while still after it's over

At home they mope: slumped, awkward, half-rebellious
Retreating to their narrow rooms and radios
They hear Little Richard, or Pat Boone covering Little Richard, on WTMJ
And take heart in the nonsense shouts, the drum set and yipping sax
Surely something will happen to them, this life in the bland debris of
    midcentury can't last
Cars, graduation, a first job at Kresge's or the canning plant
Maybe college, or eighteen months in Okinawa by a lonely sea
There will be room in the latest expansions when he gets back
Someone is planning a tract house for them on the edge of town
Schools multiply, the two-tone sedans they will want are already
    growing fins
But for now they have letter sweaters and pink change purses, and the
    hits keep coming

Winters are long here, the rink stays open from Thanksgiving through Easter
Its scratched glassy circle is a slow clock
Night after night they flicker between boredom and exquisite desire
Everyone says they're the start of something, but they aren't enough

They have no brothers and sisters, or have forgotten them

He enters into the project of his jalopy, dreaming of summer

There will be drives to the little towns nearby, evenings along the lake

They know they can get out of it all but why would they want to

Under her wool coat she is wearing a small pin shaped like a wood chip
     with his name on it

They will cling to each other because the song is ending and there are
     still good jobs in the factory

They will marry because love, oh love, swept them into the dark

V

MAGPIES

Their calls slap the air, sharper than ratchets
The necks where the sounds rise make fulcrums
Strength poised in the angle
Their legs are firm and stiff—not twigs but taut sticks
On which they pose, hop, and march
The eye giving direction, the tight beak marking the pace

What they bring to the world's eye is stark, magnificent
Black and white, blue that merges into turquoise in a fish-scale sheen
When the light hits them
No, they hit the light, they break into it
Diving from some perch high in an umbrella pine or plane tree
To scatter the glare

I saw them in a gulch near Cassis
That fire had blanched to boulders and scrub
Under the calm chestnuts in the Parque del Buen Retiro
On the damp recreation grounds by the parish church at Girton
The names of these places—exotic, European—have no value to them
The events there flat and meaningless as a map

They take their sustenance where they find it
The air for perspective, the ground for food
Anything that catches light is treasure
The fierce eye, for hunting, cannot look back
Their beauty is a perfection of purpose that continues
They will not recognize it now or when it ends

My children are grown, generations of these winged scavengers have passed
They hover in the dark behind me
Now I see them again I want to snatch them out of memory

My voice the quick beak, my language clear as theirs
Which is not chatter but warnings and commands
And knows a place not for what happened but for what its uses are

SICK SONG

When my heart was sick,
I rushed to make a song,
beneath that white window
as the rain slipped down.

I lured my sad desires
into their little rooms.
The things I couldn't do
grew fast there, thick and blurred.

When the rooms were full,
I trimmed and scrubbed the song.
I probed it like a wound,
listening for its note.

What could I hear it say
that would transpose my guilt?
Could I secrete my shame
beneath its knitting skin?

I tried it on my tongue,
I breathed it in my lungs
and went on making it
more clear, more wrong.

MAKER'S SONG

Any time I make a song
    I am not what he sings.
And when I try to sing with him
    all his beauty sinks.

I want to see him as myself
    but he is just my song.
We were as one before I felt
    this singing coming on.

Desire sent out a gleaming vine
    that drew me as it led
through curves and mesh, till beauty rose
    inside the woven hedge.

My song made him, and I became
    a creature of its will.
What new song could undermine
    the wall between us now?

FOR THE MAKERS

Peru, Moche Empire, 300 C.E.
El hombre, dónde estuvo?

They rest in the labor they gave the tomb
Helmet, nosepiece, pectoral they made for the priest and buried there
They made vessels for use, vessels for ceremony
A rich man's face, a parrot, a sea lion on a small jug
Gold goblets gleaming at the blood line
They made urns to retell their story that would never end
The binding, the bleeding, the wet ax girdling the rim
They could hold time in their hands because it was all one circle

They made what lasts, what vanished
Loincloth, thatched roof, wooden bowl they made for their needs and
    set apart
Knowing these would have no value in the other world
They made lockets for the anticoagulant, for plants of vision
Gold for the sun and silver for the moon they followed them
If they had no writing, their plans are legible
If they left no music, their songs are clear
What could their work praise but the gods who devoured it

Because they were alive, because the rains came, because corn
They made the wire-thin webs
Because war and captives, because parades, ritual abasement
They made god face, human face, beast face, mask on mask
Layers of authority marked their creation
Gold acclaimed the hierarchies
They made the miniature temple crowning the priest's scepter
Inside it, another priest holding another scepter

They were no different from others, they knew the gods drank blood
If they worshipped crabs and spiders, they found true spirit there
They saw a symmetry at the heart of things
Octopus pectoral: spider of the sea
Owl beak and eye sockets: spider of the air
They gave the priest his eight flat limbs
For the ax, for his head, for pikes, for his arms, for two legs to stand on
They incised his nosepiece with fangs

They made beads for him, strand on strand in turquoise and madrepore
They wove mica slick and glinting as obsidian
The work of their hands was a covenant with death
They arrayed the priest for his journey
Knowing their artistry would help him triumph in the other world
When dark came they slept on mats now gone to dust
They made masks, pendants, and axes
They made everything that lasts in the tomb and were lost in it

MESOAMERICAN SONG

The plant will give no seed.
    It must be sown again.
The poor line up to buy
    seeds from a bin.

Where is the long-stalk god,
    descendant of the sun,
who died and came to life
    every season?

Now the land stays dead.
    The poor man's crop will fail
unless he soaks each row
    with chemicals.

He cannot feed himself—
    a factory mills the grain
and cooks and sells it back
    to him again.

When the god drank blood
    that showed the people's love,
would he shrink away
    and let them starve?

Who captured the strict god
    who helped the people thrive?
What happened to his terror
    and his love?

THE ARCHITECTS

Ohio Valley, 200 C.E.

They took their sight lines from the tops of promontories
Their geometry from astronomers
The fixed shapes they constructed—circle, square, cut circle, octagon
Confronted the changing rivers and the forest
Their precision exalted the mind

Their plans became observatories, became calendars
Lifetimes passed into their foundations
They commanded fire, water, and the girdling of oaks
Their high earth walls and the spaced gaps between them
Set a rigorous music against the world's decay

Their eyes were fixed on the full picture
They built a measured path for the moon to follow
Their priests read stars
God was a pure angle in the circle of sky and earth
His scale the mind's scale, pointing beyond this world

If the wheel of time scored them with plagues and long winters
The perfection of their labor would deny it
Their roads, broad and raised, never wavered
The shapes they connected so vast and exact
They can only be seen fully from the sky

Now they are low hills, their symmetry muffled in grass
A softened beauty claims them in the angles of late sun
Their tongue is dirt, their descendants dispersed like mist
The shapes of their names are unknowable
Though they danced in the center of God's eye

JUNE SONG

The poplar's green abundance
reflects a simple scheme:

roots, branches, leaf on leaf—
individual parts

advancing on their own
in patterns that slowly shift

as if to one long plan.
I envy that accord.

Each opening bud repeats
the fundamental steps—

grow out to catch the light,
catch light to grow—

all in a summer's dance.
It never seems to change.

Thickening trunk that lifts
a wind harp, web of limbs

I've watched for years tell time,
you follow a strict score.

In fall your leaves will show
their true colors,

will slip the brittle twigs
and soar.

IMMEDIATE SONG

Words on a sheet,
screen in a window,
air moving in

where he doesn't move.
Still, in the quick world
he catches the light

as it slices across
the eucalyptus,
spirals of dry green

inscribing the sky.
Morning splits open.
He is taking it in:

smell of spiced dust
sharp in the old smog,
river of traffic

constant and varied,
cool hiss of sprinklers
spurting to life

just now, springs—a back door—
jay's shriek that clears out
all space around it

a moment, a moment.

ACKNOWLEDGMENTS

Grateful acknowledgment is made to the following journals in which some of the poems in this book first appeared, sometimes in different versions:

Agni: "For the Makers"
Colorado Review: "The Architects"
Consequence: "A Notebook" (as "Flags, Maps, Towers, Icons")
Hampden-Sydney Review: "Maker's Song"
Irish Pages (UK): "Return Song"
Louisville Review: "Soft Song"
Manchester Review (UK): "Our Mutual Friend"
Margie: "Care Song," "Moving Song"
Marsh Hawk Review: "Diamond Song," "Mesoamerican Song,"
    "Window Song"
New Republic: "Immediate Song"
Northwest Review: "Archaeology of 1956," "The Ice Rink"
Paris Review: "Elegies," "Promise Song"
Plume: "Flowers in a Vase"
Shenandoah: "Smart Song"
Slate: "Desks," "House"
Smartish Pace: "On Hospitals"
Stand (UK): "In the Rain," "Street, Window"
Tikkun: "Magpies"
Yale Review: "After Some Years," "A Citizen," "Sick Song"

"A Citizen" also appeared in *State of the Union: 50 Political Poems*, Joshua Beckman and Matthew Zapruder, eds., Wave Books, 2008. "Immediate Song," "June Song," "Maker's Song," "Sick Song," and "Smart Song" were set for soprano and chamber ensemble by Yehuda Yannay and first performed September 23, 2012. "Elegies" was set for chorus by Carrie Magin and first performed April 8, 2014. "Lake Song," "Soft Song," and

"Window Song" were set for mezzo soprano and piano by Steven Weimer and first performed October 26, 2015. Recordings of some of these pieces are accessible at www.donbogen.com.

I am grateful to the Camargo Foundation; the University of Cincinnati Charles Phelps Taft Research Center; the Fulbright Commissions of the United States, Spain, and the UK; and the Seamus Heaney Centre for Poetry of Queen's University, Belfast for grants that allowed me to complete this book. Cathryn Long's help at all stages was invaluable. I would also like to thank Martha Collins, James McMichael, Claudia Monpere, Donald Revell, Lisa Williams, and especially Wayne Miller for their suggestions and comments, and Daniel Slager and the great folks at Milkweed Editions for their support.

Claudia Monpere

DON BOGEN is the author of five books of poems, including *Luster* and *An Algebra*, along with a critical book on Theodore Roethke and a translation of selected poems by the contemporary Spanish poet Julio Martínez Mesanza. He has collaborated with composers from the United States and abroad. Prizes for his work include a Discovery Award and *The Writer*/Emily Dickinson Award of the Poetry Society of America, and grants from the National Endowment for the Arts and the Camargo Foundation. He has held Fulbright positions at the Seamus Heaney Centre for Poetry in Belfast and at the Universities of Santiago de Compostela and Vigo in Spain. Nathaniel Ropes Professor Emeritus at the University of Cincinnati, he serves as editor-at-large of the *Cincinnati Review* and divides his time between Cincinnati and Martinez, California.

milkweed
editions

Founded as a nonprofit organization in 1980, Milkweed
Editions is an independent publisher. Our mission is to
identify, nurture and publish transformative literature,
and build an engaged community around it.

milkweed.org

Interior design by Mary Austin Speaker
Typeset in Arno Pro

Arno Pro is an old-style serif typeface designed by Robert Slimbach for Adobe. Its design was inspired by fifteenth- and sixteenth-century typefaces, and its italic was styled after the work of Ludovico degli Arrighi, the renowned calligrapher, papal scribe, and bookseller.

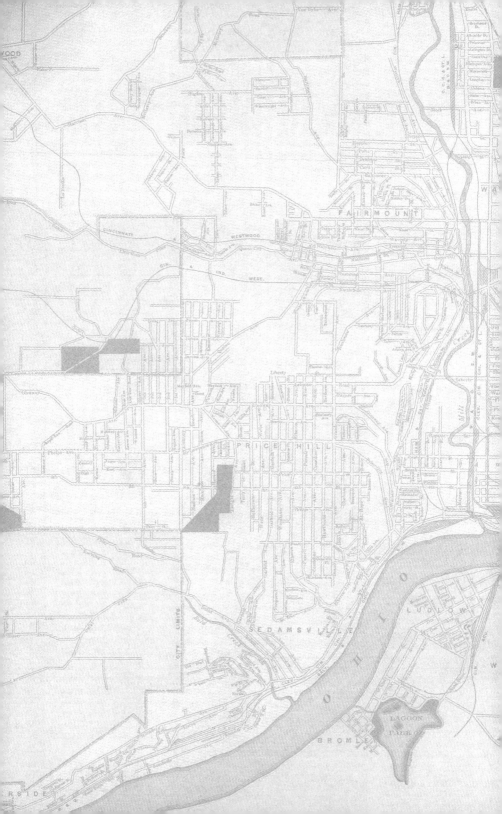